Of Love and Angels

Of Love and Angels

Poems for My Fiancée

by
Christian Alexander Barkman

Foreword by Gerard Greenway

RESOURCE *Publications* · Eugene, Oregon

OF LOVE AND ANGELS
Poems for My Fiancée

Resource Publications
An Imprint of Wipf and Stock Publishers
199 W. 8th Ave., Suite 3
Eugene, OR 97401

www.wipfandstock.com

PAPERBACK ISBN: 978-1-6667-6897-8
HARDCOVER ISBN: 978-1-6667-6898-5
EBOOK ISBN: 978-1-6667-6899-2

VERSION NUMBER 031523

For Anastasia

Contents

III -Postlude

Foreword

THROUGHOUT HISTORY THINKERS AND writers have explored the relation between Eros and Agape, the longing for romantic and sexual fulfilment and the love of God. It has been a constant theme in philosophy, theology and literature, in the western tradition and in other traditions. There can be no doubt that the two are intimately related, that, in a sense, the longing for romantic and erotic fulfilment and the longing for God are one and the same. What is understood by natural science as a basic biological urge and function is, in fact, replete with higher meaning. In this collection, Christian Alexander Barkman explores this central and profound theme in human experience and shows romantic love and the love of God as mutually revealing and supporting.

The profound affective power of romantic love reveals the beloved fully, in his or her beauty and dearness, as a sign of God's love, as an angelic figure, a messenger. No distinction can be made between body and soul. The self is released from its darkness into a new sharedness with the beloved. So intense is the enflaming of the imagination that attends romantic love in its first flush that it overflows the couple to embrace and revivify all experience of the world, glimpsed as a work of love and beauty, as the work of the love of God. It is a transformational experience and one of the most powerful sources of *caritas*, whereby we come to see that all souls are the beloveds of God and so to have proper love and compassion for them. As such, the experience of romantic love becomes a foretaste of the life to come, of the heavenly city, in which all of us will become angels in a perfect loving communion in the light of the love of God. As the lover hungers for union with the beloved, so God hungers for us. The longing of Man and the longing of God are one and the same: the longing to be fully wedded. Such is the message of *The Song of Solomon, The Song of Songs.*

The sacrament of marriage fulfils and completes the romantic union of the lovers; the couple are declared one: one body, one soul. The potential lawlessness of the erotic urge is contained in a loving and faithful pairing for life. The successful marriage is truly salvific. The couple are saved from their individual loneliness, giving each other life; building a life together as two halves of a whole. Together they suffer the many vicissitudes and trials of life. For most couples, marriage will involve the raising of a family and the extraordinary experience, and very hard work, of bringing new souls into the world.

This book about love and angels is a love-gift made by Christian for his fiancée, Anastasia – her name derives from the Greek for "resurrection." With it, Christian, still a very young man, joins a noble tradition as one of the singers of the song of songs: the song of the longing of Man and God: for all of us to be as we should be; for all of us to be together as we should. As love transforms the lovers, were this message to be heard on earth, the world would be transformed: it would become the earthly heavenly city.

I wish Christian and Anastasia all happiness in the years ahead.

—Gerard Greenway

Acknowledgements

THOUGH THIS PROJECT BEGAN under the sun of good health and good feeling, it soon followed me into darker, more difficult days. The hope and wish of presenting this gift to my fiancée has never failed however to revitalize me in those moments I needed it most. I am grateful to all the people who have encouraged and inspired me in the crafting of these poems, for they also have kept this project afloat.

To my good friend and college-mate, Kevin Akalski, who followed the development of the collection, providing himself as an editor, listener, and friend.

To Kate Clanchy, whom I was blessed with meeting in Oxford during my academic time abroad. I am grateful to Kate for her feedback and support of which she was so giving. Despite needing to return home due to persistent health issues, Kate continued to review my poetry from across the pond.

To Gerard Greenway, whom I owe the deepest of thanks. Like Kate, I met Gerard in Oxford. Being hindered by some health issues, Gerard went out of his way to accommodate me as a student of his. Gerard's generosity granted me strength to continue writing on the side of coursework. The completion of this project is in so many ways a reality because of Gerard's support. I am indebted to him for his guidance, his editing, and his feedback, and for his beautiful foreword that celebrates both the collection and my engagement. It is a blessing to have his words preceding what is so dear a project and my first creative work.

Lastly, I am grateful most of all, to my fiancée, Anastasia. She, with God, has brought me through all tempests and is the cause, the end, and the heart of these poems.

I -

Of Love

Of Love, My Task

In writing on you, my Love,
My heart alone is insufficient;
Only with the invocation of God
Do my words reach worth.

So here, with God, I etch
The blessed truth of
Our love into writing;
This grand and happy task.

And as I strive to love you
With the fervor and zeal that God does,
Though forever second to Him,
I pray that my love may mount and mount—
To the summit of dearest love.

Bundle of Miracles

A bundle of miracles
You are to me,
The most beautiful flower
You are to see.

A beacon of charity
Burning so bright,
The pearliest shooting star,
Streaking the night.

A home of comfort and warmth,
Your embrace;
A myriad delights,
Dance in your face.

Jericho

Just outside the mulish ramparts of my heart
Sounded a tiny though invincible force:
Happy and daring to find her way in,
Happy and daring and sure in her course.

Let down the gate and let me in! she cried,
Wishing for entry and wishing for trust,
I will—will—force my way in if I must!

I cried, *You are beautiful and you seem
To be true, but just who am I, to you?*
But before she could answer I resolved
To depart—into my den, into my heart.

Before long you will see how I love you
—She said with a smile. Then round
And round the tall tower she walked…
Walking around till the walls came down.

No Longer Do I Roam

Drifting off in reverie
To the tunes of princely thought,
With a limitless canvas
I was painting all I sought.
So by dream and dye I mused,
Putting heavens in the mind;
And the canvas danced and blazed!
And the canvas gleamed and shined!

I thought this was the best—
The best of dreams that could not be;
Then God showed me another,
And brought me what I could not see.
Now we are joined together,
And I count your heart my home,
In my own fancies, my own thoughts,
No longer do I roam.

Leap in My Arms, Love

When you call me by those many names,
Those names of doting, darling love attains:
My Dear, My World, My Soul, and *My Sun;*
These names you play with till you settle on one.

Then leap in my arms, Love! I know what's awaiting,
A little game of fondness you love recreating.
Jump up high, Love!—and my embrace reach,
Now strapped in my arms, we'll say our parts each:

I'm on top of the world!
You are but in my arms, Love.
But, Love, You are my world.

Your Smile, a Remedy

And how you smile is another joy,
A beautiful gift for me to enjoy.

My heart adores your smile that glows,
As witness and cure for all of my woes.

Where the Seabirds Meet

A year has passed since I was here,
fond little place I met my dear. We walk
beside the ocean blue, and hand-in-hand
discuss us two, our hopes and plans.
Meanwhile, gulls above make quite a fuss,
and though the seabirds take our quiet,
I rather like the rowdy riot;
as all the creatures by the shore, I know
give nature something more.
And I am something more today, someone
more than a year ago. Because you
hold my heart in yours—because I hold
your hand in mine.

Claimed

I feel the marble
drop into my throat.

The stitching that holds my lips
becomes unsteady;
and they tremble.

And the barb that sticks my heart
is a painful joy.

All these little tremors emerge
as a warmth lapsing within,

and then as a brutal cascade—

all the while the bell in my soul chimes,
in awe of these magical signs,

that tell that you have claimed me.

Promise Ring

Written upon gifting a promise ring before departure

I leave with you, Love, this tiny thing:
a ring of promise.

This is the first of three I will gift,
it tells to all that we commit
to a happy union 'cross sea and time—

—time, blessed in its march,
I know and trust,
though if only I could adjust…
I'd race us to the final act,
where the third of three
is placed on thee.

Illumination under Melancholy

The sharp sting of our distance
has led me into that sad place
of past memories and feelings:

when I was alone, and when my sky
had fully blackened. In that shade, the stars
did, in time, turn vibrant however,

revealing to me a ladder—
and a hallowed hand—
that pulled me up.

Now I realize, that the exodus
of my heart, from that cave
of loneliness, had taken place years ago.

There can be no further exile,
for God has joined me to Him,
and God has joined me with you.

And I remember what God
had said to me, "You are not alone,"
and remember too, what you

had said to me, with the Lord
upon your own lips,
"You are never alone."

…Thank you, Anastasia.

How Sweeter This Could Be...

Sitting here on this little bench,
A gentle breeze comes to greet me.

And soon the pleasant sun visits too,
Through a wooly window in the clouds.

Then aromas gather on the wind,
Swept from those gracious petal heads
That share nature's sweet charity

—A treasure trove of delights,
On a kind, sunny day,

But all these gifts are lacking,
While you are still away.

The Letters You Sent with Me

—Here you can find a stack of letters from my heart
Written for you for any occasion and struggles you might encounter…
I love you forever—Anastasia

I can see you writing at your desk,
With a smile in your eyes and
A smile on your lips;
With your pen happy and your heart free,
Bravely writing on your love for me.

And I can imagine the strength it took,
To wring out the words from
The sadness that smothered you.
But with tears and joy you wrote on that day,
Knowing that, for some time, I'd be away.

When you finished you bound them in a bow:
Twenty letters of your pure affection;
I bear them all now, as your craft is done,
And I feel your tender love,
In each and every one.

Entreatment

To wade through this pain
is a toil like no other. It pushes

me to some new brink
each time I take a step

and claim a calm. And
at times the prayers cast up

seem to keep me here,
perhaps to learn reliance.

Help me please,
to make it through.

Help me please,
to learn and love.

Rouse My Hopes, Love

I shudder at the present state,
Fine alabaster tainted.
How blind and unashamed we stand,
As God and history stand in judgment.

Documents thought infallible show wear;
True virtues of the past are stripped bare.
Burgeoning bureaucracy strangles like weeds,
The instinct for war re-roots and makes seed.
How can my country keep an even keel,
When hawks and hubris look on with such zeal?
They plunge and pile into the cauldron,
And plot till explosion—the deeds of the devil.

And the bile of fraud wells up the pole,
Tainting the banner and marring the soul;
And Mammon's scions send alms to high towers,
As barons forever are ripened with power;
And the nestlings, with fledgling hearts so young,
Are torn from their nests and robbed of the sun;
And in the erasure of their springtime,
No heed is paid to them.

Love, as we head this dire direction,
Rouse my hopes with your tender affection;
And be ready when the cynic creeps in,
To calm my doubts when they begin.
I trust in the promise that goodness wins,
But fret for my country and all of her sins.

God in You

Through the darkest hour,
Amid the thorns of hurt and pain,
I heard you call my name.

Now I feel you once again,
By my side in form anew,
To light, to heal, to calm, to soothe.

My Christmas Star

You are my Christmas Star!—cloaked in wonder!
—Shepherding my soul on the better path.
As my second guardian angel, Love,
You steer my spirit to heaven above.

And if ever the sinews of my ship should wear,
Repair the woodwork with your healing prayer;
And with God as rudder I shall not sink,
But rise from the waters, up from the brink.

The Bud, the Bird, and the Ram

The intent of the sprouting bud
may be cut short by the locust,

and the blackbird is felled,
at times, by the winter wind,

and the hoof of the ram
may sometimes too, fail on the crag;

but not you, my Love.
For as long as you belong

to the Lord, you will
forever be restored,

and kept for all time.

Teacher of the Heart

At every visit you run to me,
And as I look down, I still spy to see,
That same tender blush
On those same tender cheeks.

You are my greatest teacher, Love,
You are my greatest friend,
And I learn from you of love and light,
—Time and time again—

Love in Celestial Vision

In empyrean splendor this beauty was sent,
With an envoy from heaven in stellar descent—
Hardly could I distinguish 'tween the two,
As she stepped on the beam that cut through the blue.

And the kindly sun 'neath her feet did glisten,
Intent to reflect her hallowed complexion;
Then joined in brilliance her grand entourage,
To be companioned alongside the moon.

And these vicars of God, blessed at creation,
Beheld her beauty in perfect rotation.

II -

Of Angels

Of Angels and Their Beauty

How can my pen sing
The splendor of angels?
How to express such high sublimity?

If only I had a tongue like my patron:
The preaching Paduan friar—
Then I could reach an eloquence
Befitting these servants of heaven.

Lustrous saint! I pray to you!
And to the angels that surround you,
Uplift my words to nobler worth,
So that I may share in worthy poetry
The beauty of God's angels.

Lily of the Archangel

It trembled while in carriage divine,
Brought from a bed set beside heaven's pines;
The heart of the tiny lily grew yearnful,
As it sat in the palm of the archangel.

And with descent on Nazareth city,
Pangs of expectation swelled in the lily;
In journey with Gabriel to a humble home,
To tell of the wonder that was to be sown.

Then in splendor the archangel arrived,
Set before the Immaculate presence,
To whom the luminous plan was described;
These messengers bore her most pure essence.

Amidst feathered mantle of angel wing,
The lily stirred restless in Gabriel's cling;
To be here, present, in another's stead,
Roused grateful tears that wet the petal head.

Thus with tender trembling before God's chosen,
The lily bore witness to the Virgin most mild,
Who in her most blest womb would be woven,
The form and smile of the Christ Child.

Lines on Milton's Angel

The seraph Abdiel faithful found
Among the faithless, faithful only he
Among innumerable false. Unmoved,
Unshaken, unseduced, unterrified
His loyalty he kept, his love, his zeal.

    —John Milton, *Paradise Lost*

Encircled by traitors Abdiel stood;
Milton's own angel, the lone voice of good.

He paid his penance with rebuke and retreat,
And conquered bravely the devil's deceit.

And with the sea of rebel angels spurned,
To God's good graces, Abdiel returned.

And truth regained a steadfast servant,
Against the fight with the ancient serpent.

Tobias and the Angel; or,
The Book of Tobit in Seven Parts

The Context

God upon His throne is shown the prayers of two despairing souls: Tobit, whose blindness has submerged him in anguish; and Sarah, whose torment at the hands of a demon has deprived her of marriage and brought unjust reproach in both curtained gossip and brazen scorn. In answer to their pleas, God sends the archangel Raphael to heal them both. Meanwhile, Tobias, Tobit's only son, readies to leave for Media having received instruction from his father to retrieve ten talents of silver left in trust. Raphael soon after arrives; assumes a human disguise; and offers his guidance to Tobias: as with this companionship he seeks to effectuate by his mystic intervention a good outcome for all.—The angel's entrance first revealed; the journey thereafter relayed.

Part I

Alighting now from heavenly country,
The faithful archangel assumes his task:
To guide the son of pious Tobit,
And dons disguise with a corporeal mask.

So he waits outside the Nineveh home,
In the likeness of a kind young man,
Then Tobias meets him at the door—
In first fruition of the angel's plan.

His splendent wings sheathed in traveler's cloak
Artfully hides his celestial essence,
While Tobias and kin stay unaware
Of the near angelic presence.

In mortal guise he gives another name,
And as *Azariah*, greets the spousal pair,
While blind Tobit in joyful welcome,
Entrusts his son to his watchful care.

Then off to Media the boy and angel went,
As Tobit and Anna bid them safe travel,
And all the day their trek was conducted,
Until they reached the Tigris channel.

And as they set camp at evening hour,
Companionship kindled with jovial talk;
Then Tobias descended the Tigris bank,
To soak his feet from the day's arduous walk.

Then, with frightening speed, something bit his heel:
A large fish, brazen and bold!
And Tobias cried to his friend at camp,
Who called back to grab it hold.

So young Tobias hauled the fish to shore,
And brought the creature out from the river,
And the angel in turn instructed him,
To take from it the heart, gall, and liver.

Heeding his helper he set them aside
And wondered at his companion's request;
Then he ate of his catch under moon's watch
Till the curtain of night lulled him to rest.

Then the angel prayed over him in sleep;

Then took a feather from his wing and brushed
The three organs of the fish set aside—
With silent steps and movements hushed.

After the angel's mystic deed was done
He returned to his watch beside the boy,
And all the night till morning light
In watchful vigil he was employed.

Then at new day's dawn Tobias awoke,
And beheld his fellow with sleep-filled eyes,
Who beckoned him warmly for departure;
And so to the Tigris, they bade their goodbyes.

Part II

So the second day's journey they began,
And neared Media in their morning's trek;
Then Tobias asked of the fish's organs,
And inquired of their hidden effects.

So the angel divulged their curative power:
Of the gall and its touch which restores sight,
And of the heart and the liver when burned:
Which drives out bad spirits and sends them to flight.

Amazed at his companion's high knowledge,
Tobias thanked the angel in guise,
And their affable chatter renewed,
Under the sun and Median skies.

Yet as they thus pleasantly discoursed,
The angel in thought recalled his mission:
To heal in charity Tobit and Sarah—
His foremost office as God's physician.

Upon this musing he urged new topic,
And told Tobias of his spousal claim,
To the daughter of Raguel, kind Sarah,
Whose beauty and virtue he gladly named.

But Tobias countered with great unease,
In anxious remembrance of stories spread:
That told how Sarah's bridegrooms perished—
On wedding night in her bridal bed.

As by some ghastly force each groom was killed:
A covetous demon with foul intent,
To keep all men who wed Sarah from life,
As he holds her own in ceaseless torment.

In fear to leave his parents childless,
Tobias voiced dismay to the angel,
Expressing his fear of such a betrothal,
Fearing to test rumors so baneful.

But the angel in turn parried his doubt,
And gave him assurance to be not afraid,
For she was set apart for him,
Before the world was made.

So the angel gave his mystic counsel,
With instruction how to rout the demon,
And roused the hope of his hesitant friend,
Who acceded to him in faithful agreement.

Then Tobias's heart was drawn to Sarah,
And he yearned to meet her straight away;
So the angel led them in happy march onward,
To the home of Raguel without delay.

Part III

Then soon they entered Ecbatana,
The Median city of Raguel's home,
And found their man within the citadel,
Seated beside the courtyard door alone.

Then with cordial address they met Raguel,
Who matched their greeting with equal joy—
Rendering in abundance refreshment and rest,
As he led to his house the angel and boy.

With gracious welcome the two were received;
Then Raguel's wife, Edna, spoke of family ties—
And asked of her guests their relation to Tobit,
Whose answers sparked pleasant surprise.

And Tobias roused greater elation,
By declaring good Tobit his father:
Raguel heaped sweet blessings upon him,
In familial homage and kindred honor.

Following Raguel's fervent reception,
The boy and angel were invited to dine—
Edna and Sarah made ready the table,
As Raguel set out the meat and the wine.

And when the banquet was fully prepared,
The men alone reclined to eat;
Tobias watched Sarah with spousal regard,
And eyed her with fondness from his seat.

When the two women departed the room,
Tobias whispered to his helper beside,
Seeking his aid to broker the marriage,
That he may take Sarah as bride.

But Raguel heard the yearnful whisper,
And he bid Tobias not to fret—
Assuring him of his spousal right
And affirming that his claim would be met.

Following this paternal promise,
There came the grim caution in solemn lament,
As Raguel warned of seven grooms prior—
Each of them killed, without relent

But now Tobias did not heed,
And begged noble Raguel for Sarah's hand,
Who swiftly accepted the young man's plea,
And summoned his daughter with tender command.

Then Sarah was given to Tobias,
And Raguel brought their hands together,
Blessing them each with fatherly love,
And wishing their union peace forever.

Part IV

Then Edna took Sarah out of the room,
That they might make ready the bridal chamber,
While Sarah beset with harrowing worry,
Feared her new husband's life was in danger.

And at the same time, in room adjacent,
The men continued their sumptuous feast;
Then at dinner's end, Tobias was brought—
To Sarah's chamber with entry discreet.

And before he made himself known,
He took a pot of bronze and clay,
And set it on the bedside stand,
While Sarah on the bed still lay.

Into the pot he dropped the heart and liver,
The fish's organs he had taken and kept,
Then Sarah with sorrow met Tobias's eyes,
And shielded her own as she sorrowfully wept.

With gentle affection he tended to her
And taking her hand led her in prayer,
As the organs and embers in the pot,
Began to smolder and blanket the air.

And the demon in wait was repelled!
By the fumes' exorcizing effect;
And he fled the house of Raguel,
And the angel gave chase to intercept.

To desert wastes the demon took flight,
And hid his horrid wings 'neath Egypt's sands,
Though hardly did his cover conceal him—
Unearthed as he was by the angel's hands.

With effortless force the angel bound him:
Both hand and foot to a pillar of stone;
Then the angel departed from him,
And the demon wailed on in ceaseless groan.

As Tobias and Sarah finished their prayer
The angel likewise returned from flight,
Having answered their plea and God's command:
To secure their safety that night.

Soon after the couple passed into sleep,
Raguel attended his gloomy labor,
And dug a grave in sad expectation,
That Tobias had died in the chamber.

And at the completion of his bleak task,
He sent a maid to check on the room—
Who reported back with joyous news,
That Tobias had escaped what seemed certain doom.

And Raguel thanked God in ecstatic praise,
For His great mercy upon the couple,
And ordered his servants to fill in the grave,
Before dawn's break with spade and shovel.

Part V

And when the pair of newlyweds waked,
They embraced each other in glad relief—
Sarah wept her happy tears,
Witness to her conquered grief.

And then Tobias rose from bed,
In heedful answer to Raguel's call,
And he gave his wife a parting kiss,
Then met her father in the hall.

Upon appearing Raguel clasped him tight,
And proclaimed that he was now his father;
And he bid him stay for fourteen days,
For a marriage celebration proper.

But when the fourteen days had passed,
Tobias insisted he must return:
Back to his father and mother at home,
Who both now waited in anxious concern.

So Raguel and Edna wished him farewell
And entrusted their daughter to his care,
Then praised the marriage once more with joy,
And blessed their journey in loving prayer.

So Azariah came before them both,
And conducted them back to Tobit's house;
Thus Tobias followed his angel guide—
In happy return with Sarah his spouse.

And when the three drew near to Nineveh,
The angel told Sarah to walk behind;
That he and Tobias might go ahead,
To make things ready before she arrived.

So in eager dash Tobias went onwards,
With his mystic helper in swifter pace,
Who told him to have ready the gall,
As they approached his father's place.

Part VI

Upon arrival Anna met them—
And embraced her son in tender concern;
But maternal worry passed away,
With the joy of her son's return.

And then blind Tobit emerged from the house,
With stumbling steps upborne by a cane;
And though he ached to see his son,
His sight met darkness in futile strain.

Then the angel directed Tobias
To apply the gall they had preserved,
Upon the eyelids of Tobit—
That his vision of shadows might be purged.

So Tobias came before his father
And smeared the gall upon each eye;
Then Tobit's world suffused with light,
And he wept in joyous cry—

"I see you, my son, the light of my eyes!
Blessed be God!—and bless His Holy Name!"
Then he went to meet Sarah at Nineveh's gate,
Shouting and rejoicing with passion aflame.

And when he met her he blessed her with joy,
And declared her his daughter in joyous cheer;
Then embraced her beside his son and wife,
And in paternal fold held them all dear.

While Azariah watched the happy scene,
A glad smile stretched his saintly face;
By his aid, good hearts were unburdened—
Heaven stooped to bestow God's grace.

Then Tobit announced the wedding feast,
And in haste began the preparations,
And Nineveh observed for seven days—
The blithe and happy celebrations.

Part VII

At the end of the week-long merriment,
When gifts had been given and drinks had been drained,
Azariah called Tobit and his son,
And in hidden counsel thus proclaimed—

"Bless God!—bless and sing praises to His Name!
Never forget what He has done for you,
And never be slow to acknowledge Him;
All praise and glory to Him is due.

Let good, not gold, be your greater stock,
So that evil does not overtake you;
And when ills and worries beset your lives,
Obtain in prayer hope anew."

And when Azariah concluded,
He at last let fall his human disguise;
And before his form and radiant light,
Tobias and Tobit gaped in surprise.

Then from that mighty frame the voice was renewed,
And told his true identity:
Raphael, whose name among angels,
Is garbed in high ascendancy.

"It was I who brought your prayers before God,
And read before Him your plea and record.
I am Raphael, one of the seven
Who comes before the glory of the Lord.

Peace be with you and do not be afraid,
But stand and acknowledge God in your hearts;
And write down all that you have seen—
And all the graces God imparts."

So Tobias and Tobit rose with zeal,
And blessed God in adoring praise;
Then Raphael withdrew himself,
And left them in their upward gaze.

And looking up the two did see,
The angel in his rapid flight—
Returning to his home above,
Vanishing from their happy sight.

Ancient of Days

Thrones were placed,
and the Ancient of days sat:
his garment was white as snow,
and the hair of his head like clean wool:
his throne like flames of fire:
the wheels of it like a burning fire.
A swift stream of fire issued forth from before him:
thousands of thousands ministered to him,
and ten thousand times a hundred thousand
stood before him.

    —Daniel 7:9–10

He is the *Ancient of Days*,
Evermore and without birth;
He sets His eternal gaze—
Across the ends of the earth.

He is the *Ancient One*,
Upon the Throne of endless grace;
Angel and man are both His sons—
His likeness shines in each their face.

Regent of the Sun

And God ignited the hull of the sun,
And placed the wise Uriel as regent:
That noble archangel who had won,
Charge over sky by God's good agreement.

In rapt delight and with dutiful sight
Uriel's eye hangs over the heavens,
With whole devotion to the grand task to
Watch and minister the thoughtful motion
Of celestial bodies. Within the hull
Of the sun, the sage archangel stirs; here,
He employs his angelic science and
With holy instruments, steers the stars on
Their mystic course. Here, lofted above thin
Mortal purview, God's astronomy is
Conducted, as Uriel brings planet
And star under teleologic current.
From prodigious height above our earthly
Sphere, he mediates the astral court and
Records all measurements cosmic; and as
One of the seven who stand before the
Lord on special charge and heightened mission,
He waits with ready wing to hasten to
Almighty Godhead. And all these duties
He attends, alongside watch over seat
Of man—this task his chief delight. Thus from
Observatory divine, his seraph
Eye lay fixed, and beholds in captivation
The face of the Creator within the
Face of man, and gladdens at those good souls
Who keep their focus heavenward. Though mixed

Along with glad regard stirs sorrow too,
And moves at times his firm archangelic
Brow to solemn countenance; for to view
Souls myriad scattered far from the light
And hope of heaven, in doubtful wander
And godless exile self-imposed, brings
Sadness to the saintly watchman. Thus, from
In his blazing chamber, he endeavors
To alter the wayward from their sightless
Path, and through majestic inspiration,
Impels their vision upward—to the birds
At midheaven in wondrous flight, and to
The stars in stellar glow that illumine
The night. And to the sun, his radiant
Seat, he too prompts gaze and awe, not to draw
Worship, but to guide devotion higher—
Past sky and star to shared Father above,
True country of man and fullness of love.

Before the Throne

An Interpretation of the Cherubim

Now the cherubim emerge—
And they hang before the Throne,
Wearing garments white as snow.

They resemble man in face and form;
And have four wings that glow
In the presence of the Lord's Seat.

From their back rise two wings,
Two more descend to cover their legs;
They have feet like an ox,
Gold shoes fit their hooves.

With the subtlest strain of their wings, there is thundering.
They clasp in their hands lightning bolts,
For the Lord has given them power over storms.

They wear crowns of shining silver,
Within each crown shine four colored jewels:
Of gold, of blue, of red, of white—
Each jewel ablaze in a brilliant light.

First, there is the golden flame—
And in its gleam, the image of a lion;
A great scar is on its face
And it sits upon a rock.

Beside it burns the bluish flame—
And in its glow, there is an eagle;
It carries in its beak a branch
And its wings are wide outspread.

Then there is the crimson flame—
And in its flicker, there is an ox;
Nails are in its hooves
And it pulls a cart of wheat.

The last flame is white—
And in its light, there is the image of a *man*;
His face is meek, and his eyes are bright;
He holds a book in his left hand
And his right arm is outstretched.
The white flame blazes above the cherub's head,
And it mingles with the other flames atop its crown—

And the lesser angels contemplate
The revelation within these fires,
Imparted by the cherubim choirs.

First to Announce, First to Adore

Thine the first worship was, when gloom
Through heaven's thinned ranks did move,
Thus giving unto God the bloom
Of young creation's love.

    —Frederick William Faber, "Hail, Bright Archangel!
    Prince of Heaven"

Into scabbard he sheaths his mighty sword:
The hallowed arms that felled the wicked horde;
As against vast legions he did contend,
The glory of God he fought to defend,
From the haughty boast of apostate crew,
Who sought high power in pernicious coup.
Now with sword sheathed, he stoops on bended knee,
And waits in reverence, new charge or decree.

Then a glorious presence to him came near,
And he readied in turn his obedient ear.
The light from the figure beamed so intense,
It overwhelmed his angelic sense;
And in the center of this great light—
A form like his maker in virtue and might:
Equal in glory, equal in power,
Yet to don flesh this premature hour.

And as heaven's choirs trumpeted song,
The voice from the figure pierced through the throng,
And honored him for his adoration
To the plan God showed in revelation;
Then gave him new name, and called him *Michael*:

The battle cry of the first disciple,
Who was first to announce, and first to adore,
The sacred humanity of our dear Lord.

The Lamb Triumphant

Come and see the lamb triumphant!
Come and see his wondrous light!
Come and see his cloven hooves,
  That won for him the fight.

Behold the horns that jut his head,
Seven peaks of kingly power,
Amid his host on harp and lyre,
  Unceasing at this hour.

Come and glimpse his noble gaze,
Upon the dawn of endless peace;
Seven eyes with burning flames,
  Within his luminous fleece.

Behold the white steeds at his back,
Mounted by angelic servants,
As heaven's armies victorious,
  Bow in awed observance.

Come and see the final triumph!
Come and see this perfect sight!
The King of kings, and Lord of lords,
  Has won for us eternal light.

III -

Postlude

And from the blessed power that rolls
About, below, above;
We'll frame the measure of our souls,
They shall be tuned to love.

—William Wordsworth, "Lines Written at
a small distance from my House"

An Epigraph on Chrysostom

*I courted you, and I love you, and prefer
you to my own soul. For the present life
is nothing. And I pray, and beseech, and
do all I can, that we may be counted
worthy so to live this present life, as that
we may be able also there in the world
to come to be united to one another in
perfect security. For our time here is
brief and fleeting. But if we shall be
counted worthy by having pleased God
to so exchange this life for that one,
then shall we ever be both with Christ
and with each other, with more abundant
pleasure. I value your affection above all
things, and nothing is so bitter or so
painful to me, as ever to be at variance
with you.*

    —St. John Chrysostom, *Homily 20 (on Ephesians)*

You are my dearer half
And truest home till heaven,
I've placed this lengthy epigraph,
To share its best expression
—Best on love and best on marriage,
Chrysostom's words pull holy's carriage;
From saintly mouths flow lovely things,
I pray such love to you I bring.

Matrimony

The liturgical act;
the covenant pact;

then at last my dear wife.
That new daybreak of life—

can hardly wait!